This book is a special gift for

_____

From: _____

Date: _____

This book is dedicated
to my grandchildren,
Aidan, McKenna, and Dylan
- who love to learn.

DR. C'S
COOL CLUES
AND CARTOONS

The Presidents

Jerry Cavanaugh

Dr. C's Cool Clues and Cartoons: The Presidents

By Jerry Cavanaugh

AimHi Press
Orlando, Florida
AimHiPress.com
©2021, Jerry Cavanaugh

Names: Cavanaugh, Jerry, Author and Illustrator. | Traynor, Daniel, Cover and Layout.

Title: Dr. C's Cool Clues and Cartoons: The Presidents / by Jerry Cavanaugh

Description: Orlando, FL | AimHi Press, 2021. | Summary: How many of these quirky quiz trivia questions can you guess about the United States Presidents?

Identifiers: Library of Congress Control Number:

2021937219 (print) | ISBN 978-1-945493-42-3 (paperback)

Subjects: CYAC: Trivia. | Presidents. | US History. | Education. |

Classification: LCC PZ7.1.C38 Cav 2021(Print)

LC record available at https://lccn.loc.gov/2019940825

How to use Dr. C's Cool Clues and Cartoons:

Select the answer you believe is correct,
then turn the page to find out if you're right.
Use the Scoresheet on the last page
to keep track of your score.

1. What president had a pet raccoon?

A Theodore Roosevelt

B Richard Nixon

C Harry Truman

D Calvin Coolidge

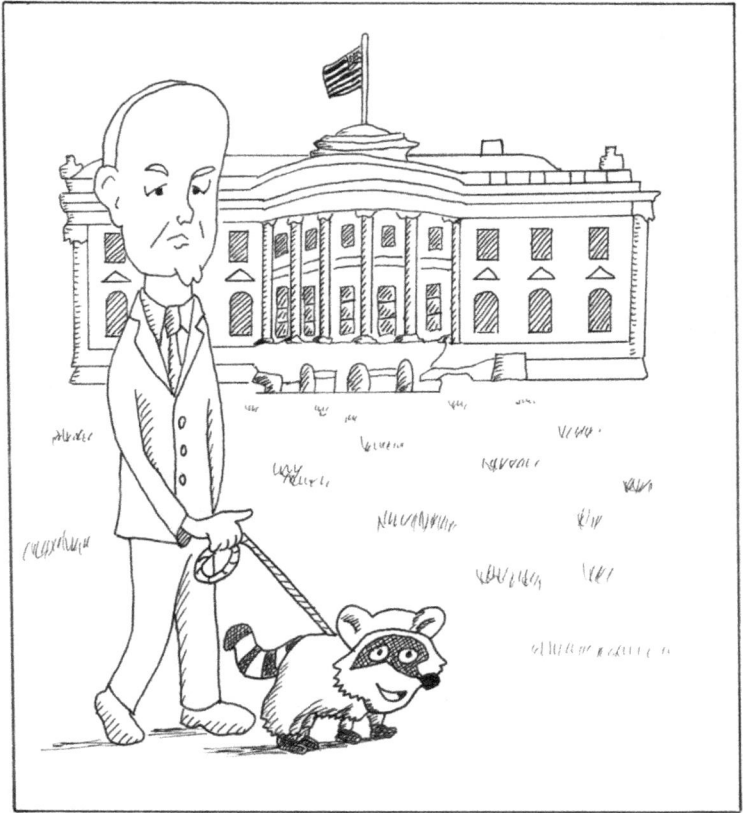

Answer: D

President Coolidge and his wife, Grace, received Rebecca the raccoon as a gift in 1926 from friends in Mississippi. They kept her on a leash when outside, but inside she had the run of the White House. Her favorite foods were shrimp, persimmons, and eggs.

4

2. Who was the only president who never married?

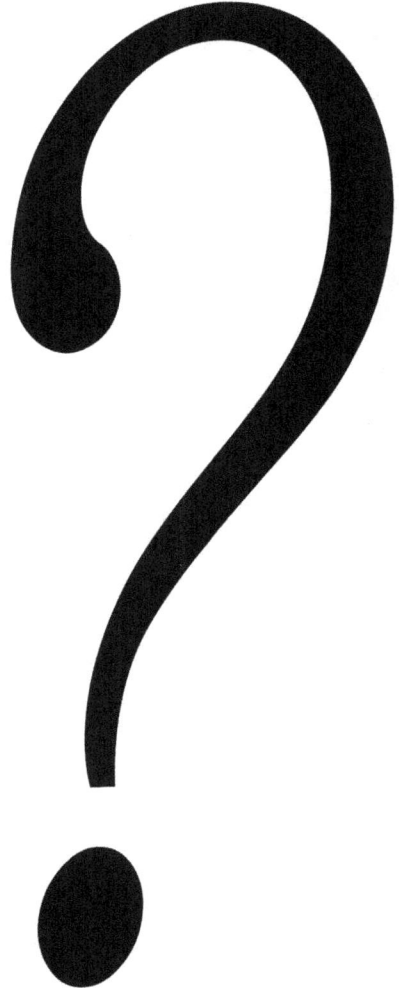

A Millard Fillmore

B Martin Van Buren

C James Buchanan

D Zachary Taylor

Answer: C

Buchanan was engaged to marry Ann Caroline Coleman, but after she died, he was too heartbroken to ever consider marriage again.

3. *What singer did Richard Nixon make an honorary agent of the Federal Bureau of Narcotics and Dangerous Drugs?*

A Buddy Holly

B Pat Boone

C Chuck Berry

D Elvis Presley

Answer: C

In December 1970, President Nixon named Elvis Presley an honorary agent of the Federal Bureau of Narcotics and Dangerous Drugs in a ceremony at the White House.

4. *What president was so religious that he attended services every Sunday at three different churches?*

A Thomas Jefferson

B John Quincy Adams

C Millard Fillmore

D James Monroe

B

Answer:

Although a member of the Unitarian faith, John Quincy Adams also regularly attended Presbyterian and Episcopalian services, often on the same Sunday. He read the Bible for at least an hour every morning.

5. Who is the only president who earned a PhD?

A John Quincy Adams

B Woodrow Wilson

C James A. Garfield

D Bill Clinton

Answer:

Woodrow Wilson received a PhD in government from Johns Hopkins University in 1886.

6. What president was part owner of the Texas Rangers baseball team?

A Ronald Reagan

B Jimmy Carter

C George W. Bush

D Lyndon Johnson

George W. Bush bought a part ownership of the Texas Rangers in April 1989 for approximately $600,000. He sold his share of the team in 1998 for $14,900,000.

7. Who was the only president who attended medical school?

A John Adams

B Andrew Johnson

C Rutherford B. Hayes

D William Henry Harrison

Answer:

William Henry Harrison studied
medicine in 1891 at Richmond, Virginia,
and Philadelphia, Pennsylvania, but
never earned a medical degree.
He left school in November of that
year to enlist in the army after the
death of his father.

8. Who is the only president who has an asteroid named after him?

A George Washington

B Franklin D. Roosevelt

C Abraham Lincoln

D Herbert Hoover

In March, 1920, Austrian astronomer Johann Palisa of the University of Vienna, discovered an asteroid, which he named "Hooveria" in honor of Herbert Hoover, who at the time was supervising relief efforts in Europe following the First World War.

9. Which president got married at the youngest age?

A Andrew Jackson

B Franklin Pierce

C Andrew Johnson

D James K. Polk

Answer: C

Andrew Johnson was only 18 years old when he married Eliza McCardle on May 17, 1827 in Greeneville, Tennessee. They remained married for 48 years.

10. *What president once worked as a park ranger in Yellowstone National Park?*

A Theodore Roosevelt

B John F. Kennedy

C William Howard Taft

D Gerald Ford

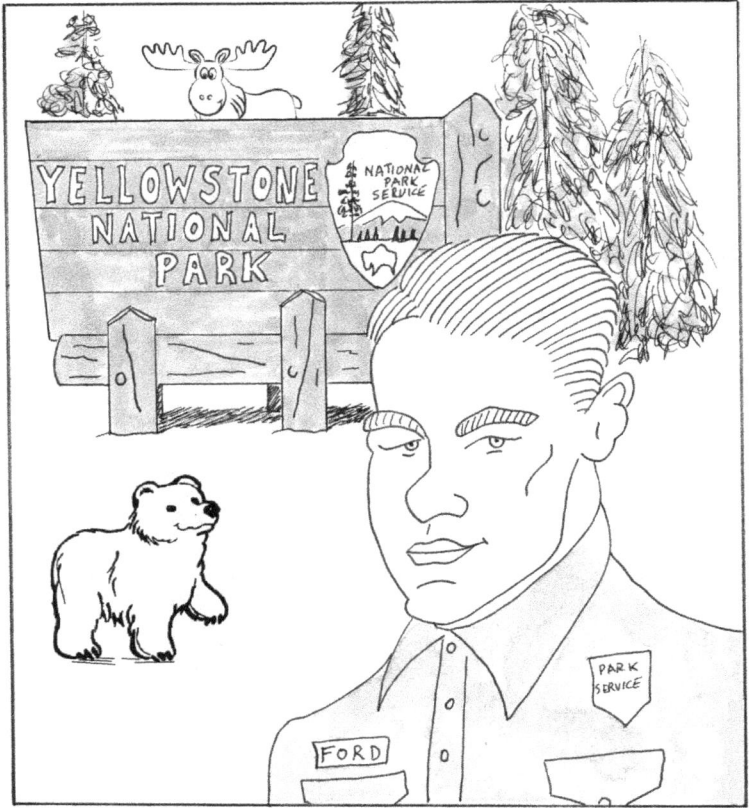

During the summer of 1936, Gerald Ford served as a seasonal park ranger at Yellowstone and recalled it as "one of the greatest summers of my life."

11. Theodore Roosevelt's daughter, Alice, had a unique pet named "Emily Spinach." What kind of animal was it?

A An ocelot

B A snake

C An ostrich

D A skunk

Answer:

Alice, who was 17 when her father began his presidency in 1901, also had two dogs: a long-haired chihuahua named Leo and a small black Pekinese named Manchu, who she got on a trip to China.

12. Who was the only president who had been a Rhodes Scholar?

A Woodrow Wilson

B Bill Clinton

C Franklin D. Roosevelt

D George W. Bush

B

Answer:

After graduating from Georgetown University in 1968 with a Bachelor's Degree in international affairs, Bill Clinton received a Rhodes Scholarship to study at the University of Oxford in England.

13. Who was the first president to ever attend a major league baseball game?

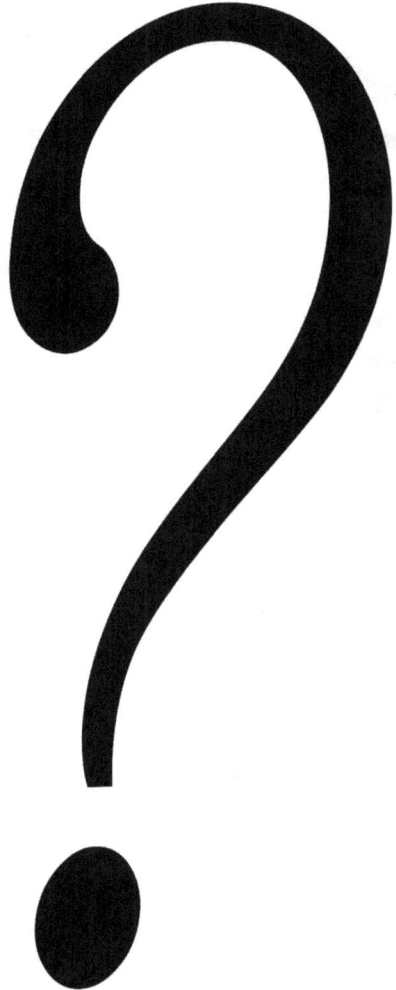

A Theodore Roosevelt

B Grover Cleveland

C Benjamin Harrison

D Calvin Coolidge

On June 2, 1892, President Benjamin Harrison attended a game between the Cincinnati Reds and the Washington Senators at Boundary Field, two blocks from the White House (Cincinnati won, 7 to 4).

14. *What president had a pet parrot whose language was so foul that it had to be removed from that president's funeral so the attendees wouldn't be offended?*

A John Quincy Adams

B James Buchanan

C Andrew Jackson

D Richard Nixon

When Andrew Jackson died in 1845, his pet parrot, Poll, had to be removed from the funeral because his repeated bursts of foul language upset the 3000 mourners who had gathered for the ceremony at The Hermitage in Tennessee.

15. Who was the first president licensed to fly an airplane?

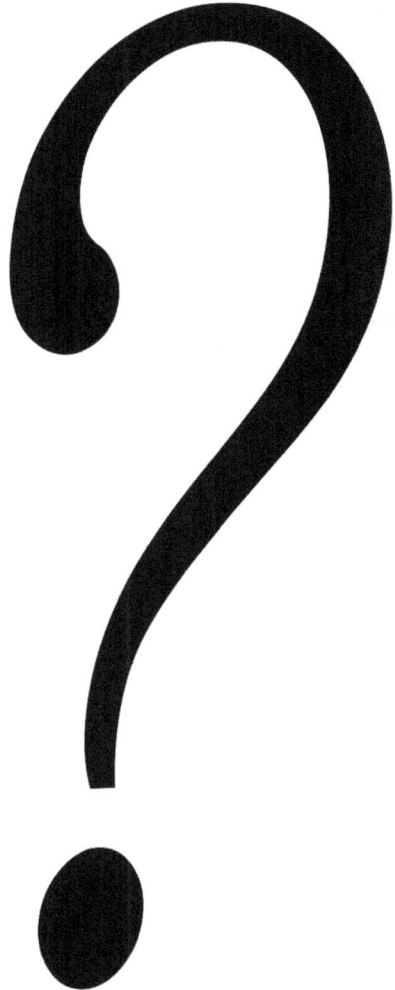

A Dwight Eisenhower

B George H.W. Bush

C Richard Nixon

D George W. Bush

Dwight Eisenhower received his private pilot's license in July 1939, while serving in the Army in the Philippines.

16. Which president's hobby was stamp collecting?

A Woodrow Wilson

B Franklin D. Roosevelt

C Herbert Hoover

D Jimmy Carter

B

Answer:

Franklin D. Roosevelt started collecting stamps as a child. After his death in 1945, his collection was sold at auction for $230,000.

17. *What president once held a yard sale on the White House lawn?*

A Chester Alan Arthur

B Warren G. Harding

C Herbert Hoover

D Harry Truman

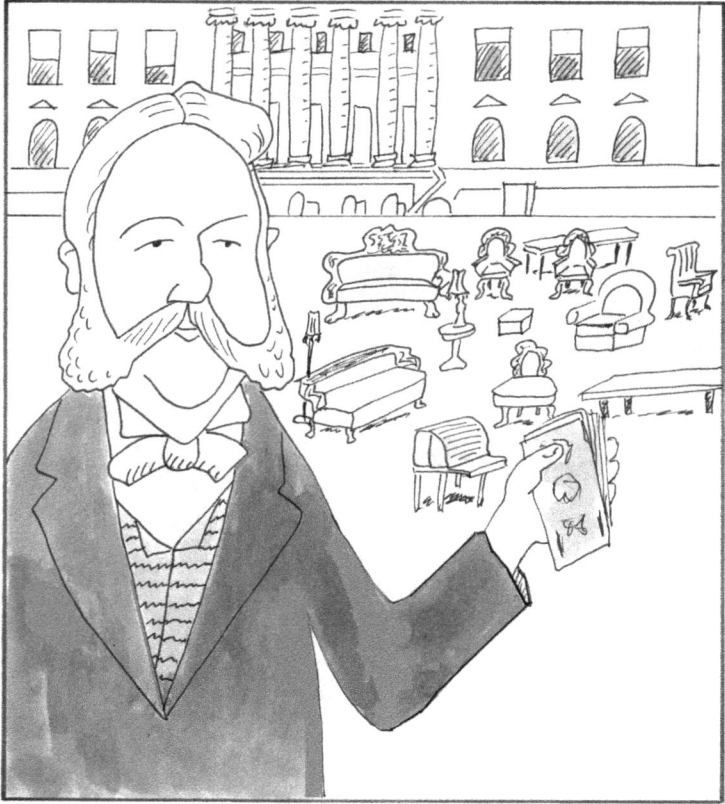

Answer:

In 1881, President Chester Alan Arthur held a yard sale on the White House lawn, in which he raised $8,000 from the sale of 25 wagon loads of furniture and clothing that had been accumulated over the years in the presidential mansion.

18. When James Madison was a student at Princeton, what was his major course of study?

A Hebrew

B History

C English

D Political Science

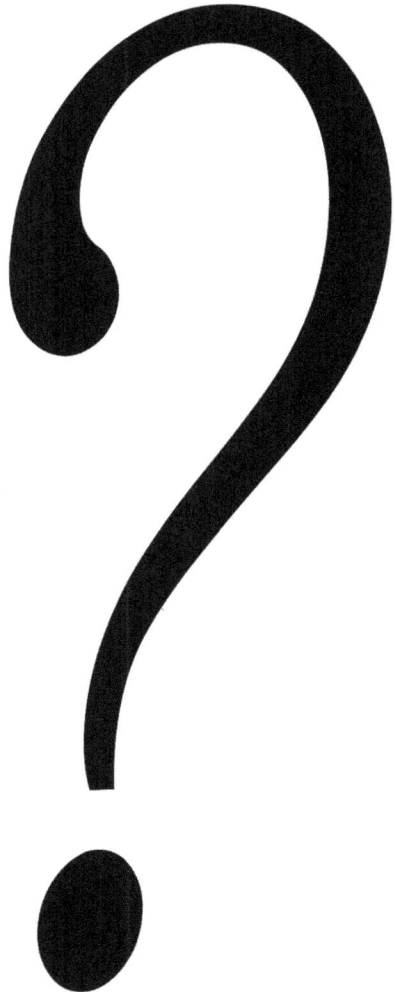

Answer:

מִי שֶׁבֵּרַךְ אֲבוֹתֵינוּ אַבְרָהָם יִצְחָק וְיַעֲקֹב הוּא יְבָרֵךְ אֶת
חַיָּלֵי צְבָא הֲגַנָּה לְיִשְׂרָאֵל, הָעוֹמְדִים עַל מִשְׁמַר אַרְצֵנוּ
וְעָרֵי אֱלֹהֵינוּ מִגְּבוּל הַלְּבָנוֹן וְעַד מִדְבַּר מִצְרַיִם וּמִן הַיָּם
הַגָּדוֹל עַד לְבוֹא הָעֲרָבָה בַּיַּבָּשָׁה בָּאֲוִיר וּבַיָּם. יִתֵּן יהוה

מִי שֶׁבֵּרַךְ אֲבוֹת
חַיָּלֵי צְבָא הֲגַנָּה
וְעָרֵי אֱלֹהֵינוּ מִגְ
הַגָּדוֹל עַד לְבוֹא
אֶת אוֹיְבֵינוּ הַקָּמ
הוּא יִשְׁמֹר וְיַצִּיל
וּמַחֲלָה וְיִשְׁלַח בְּרָ
שׂוֹנְאֵינוּ תַּחְתֵּיהֶם
וִיקַיֵּם בָּהֶם הַכָּתוּב
לָכֶם עִם אִיְבֵיכֶם

James Madison's major at Princeton
was Hebrew, which was a required
course of study in many American
colonial colleges.

19. Who was the first Boy Scout to become president?

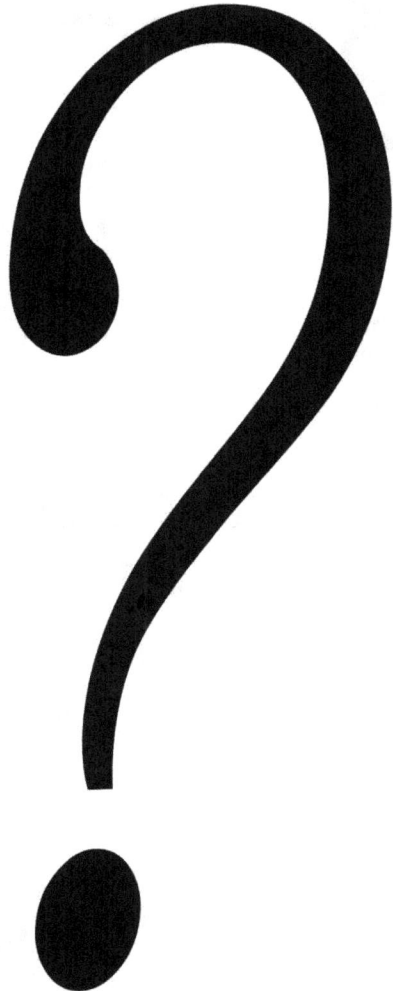

A Theodore Roosevelt

B Gerald Ford

C John F. Kennedy

D Jimmy Carter

In 1929, at the age of twelve,
John F. Kennedy joined Boy Scout
Troop 2 in Bronxville, New York.
He remained in the troop until 1931.

20. *What First Lady brought the first cherry blossom trees to Washington, D.C. from Japan?*

A Edith Roosevelt

B Lady Bird Johnson

C Eleanor Roosevelt

D Helen "Nellie" Taft

In 1912, Helen "Nellie" Taft planted the first cherry blossom trees in Washington. They had been donated by the Japanese ambassador to the United States.

21. Who was the only president born in New Hampshire?

A Calvin Coolidge

B James Buchanan

C James K. Polk

D Franklin Pierce

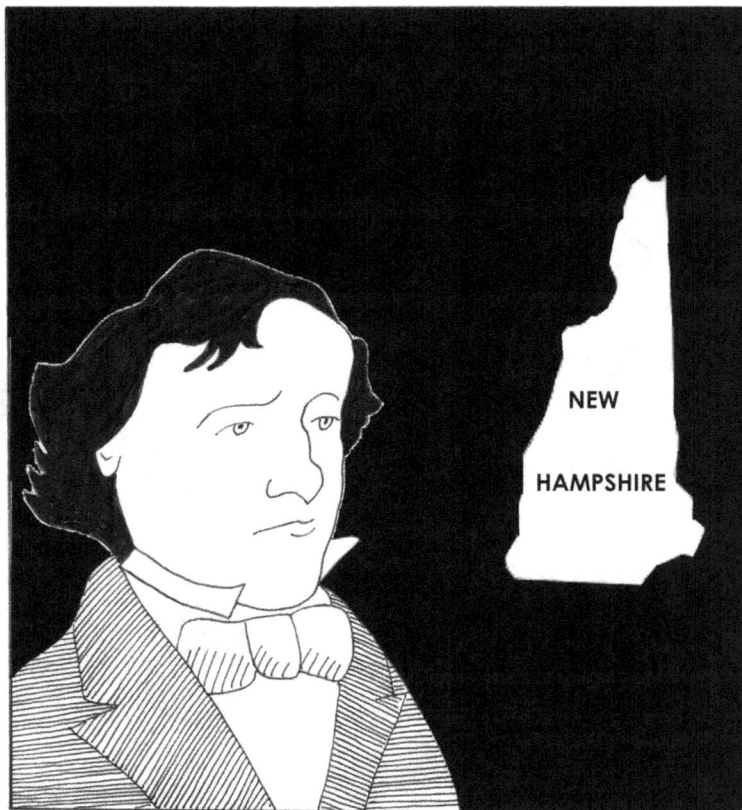

Answer: D

Pierce was born in Hillsborough,
New Hampshire, on November 3, 1804.

22. What First Lady was the first president's wife with a college degree?

A Julia Dent Grant

B Jackie Kennedy

C Lucy Webb Hayes

D Hillary Clinton

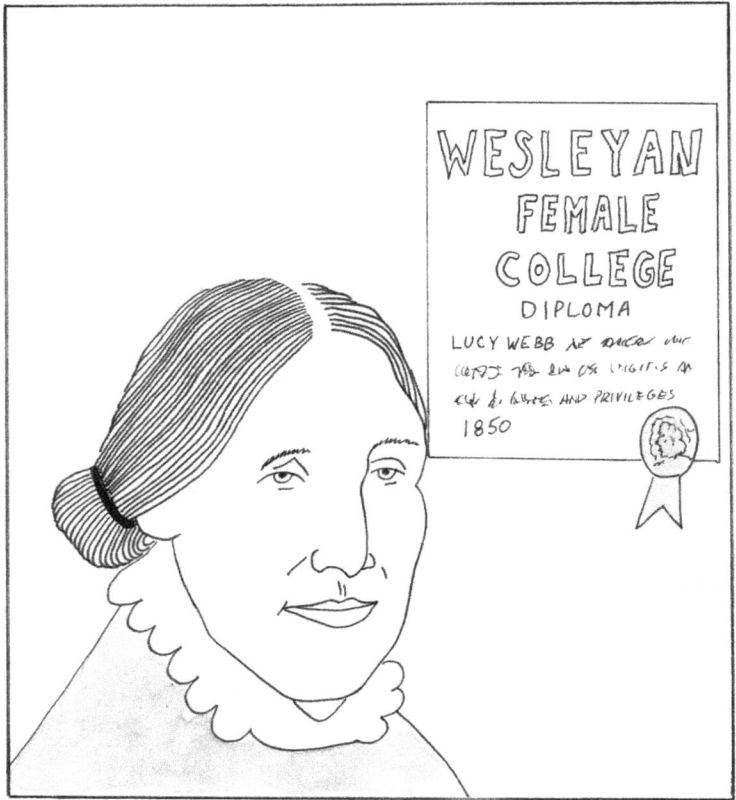

Lucy Webb graduated from Cincinnati Wesleyan Female College in 1850. Her commencement essay was entitled, "The Influence of Christianity on National Prosperity." She married Rutherford B. Hayes two years later.

23. **What future president spent his summers as a lifeguard on a beach by a river in Illinois?**

A Ronald Reagan

B Barack Obama

C Abraham Lincoln

D Ulysses S. Grant

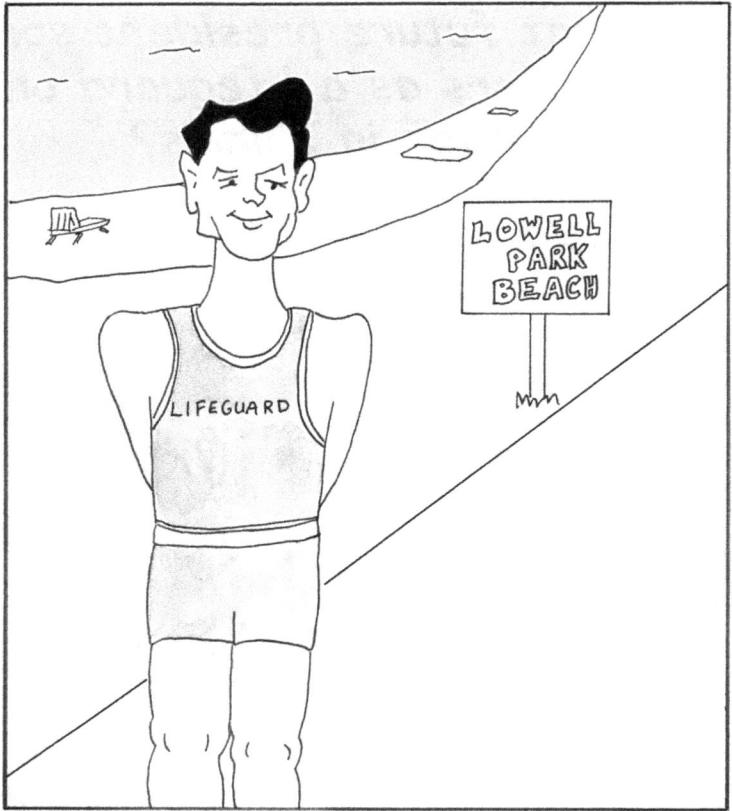

From 1927 until 1932, Ronald Reagan was a lifeguard in the summer at Lowell Park near his home town of Dixon, Illinois. He was credited with saving 77 people from drowning.

24. **What president once received a patent for an invention that lifted boats over sandbars using large air-filled bags?**

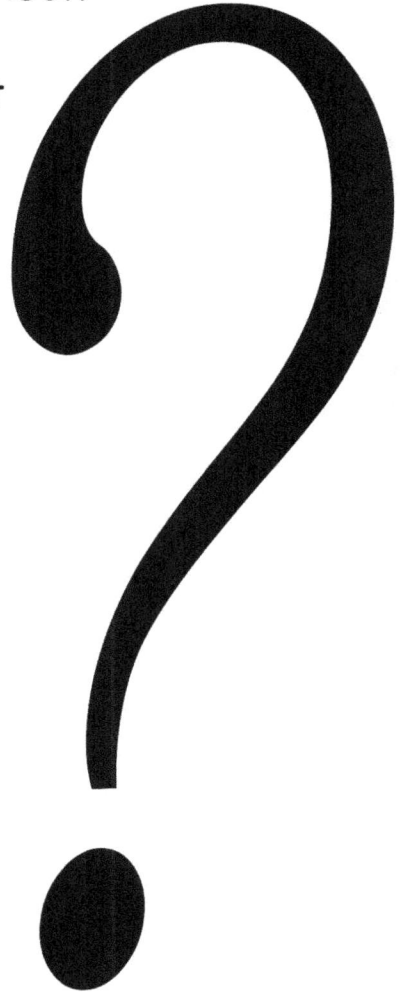

A William Henry Harrison

B Theodore Roosevelt

C Zachary Taylor

D Abraham Lincoln

Answer: D

On May 22, 1849, Abraham Lincoln received Patent No. 6469, for a device that would lift boats over river sandbars. The invention was never built, but he is still the only president who ever got a patent for an invention.

25. Which one of these presidents played the harmonica?

A Theodore Roosevelt

B Richard Nixon

C Calvin Coolidge

D Harry Truman

Answer: C

According to his biographers, President Coolidge liked to sit in his rocking chair on the White House porch and play his harmonica.

26. Who is the only president who earned degrees from both Yale and Harvard?

A Jimmy Carter

B George W. Bush

C Bill Clinton

D Woodrow Wilson

In 1968, George W. Bush earned a Bachelor's Degree in history from Yale. He earned a Masters in Business Administration (MBA) from Harvard in 1975.

27. What president had a bowling alley installed in the White House?

A Harry Truman

B Richard Nixon

C Herbert Hoover

D Lyndon Johnson

B

Answer:

In 1969, President Nixon had a one-lane bowling alley built beneath the driveway leading to the North Portico of the White House.
Both he and Mrs. Nixon were avid bowlers and used the lane frequently.

28. What president had two tiger cubs he kept as pets for a while?

A Andrew Jackson

B Ulysses S. Grant

C William Howard Taft

D Martin Van Buren

Answer: D

Shortly after taking office in 1837, President Van Buren received two tiger cubs as a gift from Kabul al Said, the Sultan of Oman. Although Van Buren wanted to keep them, Congress claimed they belonged to the country, so, after being kept for a short time in the White House, the cubs were sent to a zoo.

29. What president was the first to install solar panels on the roof of the White House?

A Jimmy Carter

B Ronald Reagan

C Barack Obama

D Bill Clinton

Answer:

In 1979, President Carter ordered that solar panels be installed on the White House roof to supplement the mansion's electrical supply. In 1981, President Reagan had them removed, but President Obama had them reinstalled in 2010.

30. **What president used to exercise by juggling weights know as Indian clubs?**

A James A. Garfield

B Warren G. Harding

C Woodrow Wilson

D Dwight Eisenhower

Answer:

To build muscle and stay in shape, President Garfield juggled Indian clubs (which resembled bowling pins) swinging them in patterns as part of an exercise routine.

31. Who was the first daughter of a U.S. president to get married at the White House?

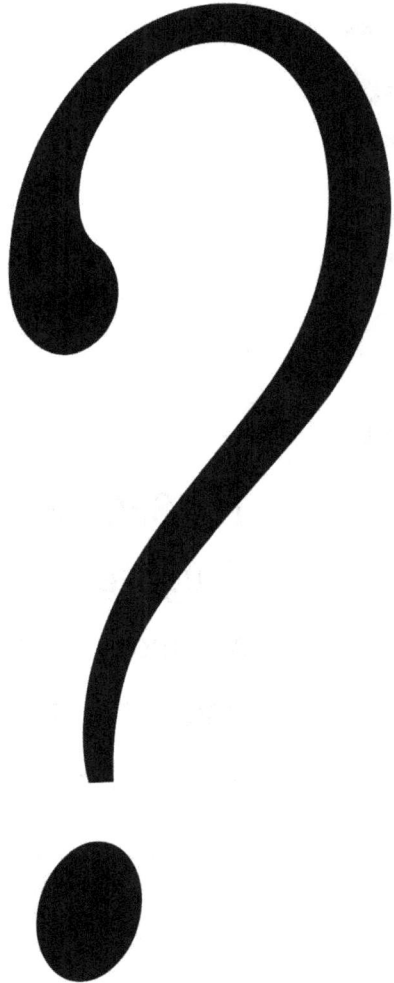

A Jenna Bush

B Maria Monroe

C Alice Roosevelt

D Caroline Kennedy

B

Answer:

In 1820, Maria Hester Monroe, daughter of James and Elizabeth Monroe, became the first president's daughter to be married in the White House when she wed Samuel L. Gouverneur.

32. Thomas Jefferson was said to have introduced what type of food to the United States?

A Cinnamon Buns

B Ice Cream

C Pasta

D Borscht

Answer: C

Jefferson served a macaroni and cheese casserole at a White House dinner on February 6, 1802. It was said to be the first time Americans had ever seen pasta.

33. *Who was the first president whose voice was broadcast over the radio?*

A Woodrow Wilson

B Warren G. Harding

C Herbert Hoover

D Franklin D. Roosevelt

B

Answer:

On June 14, 1922, President Harding
was addressing in crowd at a celebration
honoring Francis Scott Key, composer
of "The Star-Spangled Banner," when
his voice was transmitted by radio.
It would be another three years, however,
before a president (Coolidge) would
deliver an address specifically designed
for a radio audience.

34. What First Lady was the only one to serve as a United States senator?

A Hillary Clinton

B Jackie Kennedy

C Eleanor Roosevelt

D Lady Bird Johnson

Answer:

Hillary Rodham Clinton was elected to the U.S. Senate from New York in 2000 and re-elected in 2006. She resigned from her Senate seat in January, 2009, to become secretary of state in the Obama administration.

35. What president had a son who had a regular role on the daytime TV soap opera, "The Young and the Restless?"

A Gerald Ford

B Ronald Reagan

C Richard Nixon

D Donald J. Trump

Answer:

A

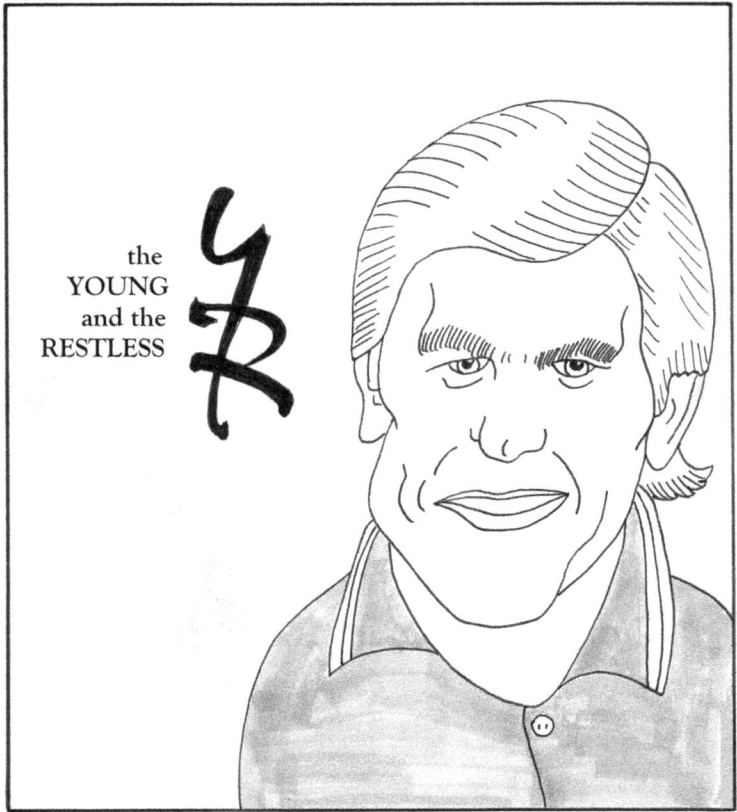

the
YOUNG
and the
RESTLESS

Steven Ford, son of Gerald and Betty Ford, played the role of private investigator Andy Richards on the show from 1981 to 1987, and again briefly in 2002-2003.

36. Benjamin and Caroline Harrison lived in the White House when what modern convenience was first installed in that home?

A Central heating

B Electric lights

C The Internet

D Running water

Answer:

In 1891, the Edison Company installed the first electric lights in the White House. President Benjamin Harrison and First Lady Caroline Harrison refused to touch the light switches for fear of electrocution.

37. *What president once served as the sheriff of Erie County, New York?*

A Franklin Pierce

B Theodore Roosevelt

C Grover Cleveland

D Millard Fillmore

Answer: C

Grover Cleveland served as the sheriff of Erie County, New York, (where Buffalo is located) from 1871 to 1873.

38. **What First Lady was the first woman in the United States to earn a college degree in geology?**

A Lucy Webb Hayes

B Edith Wilson

C Abigail Fillmore

D Lou Hoover

Answer: D

In 1898, Lou Henry graduated from Stanford University with a Bachelor's Degree in geology, the first woman in the United States to earn a degree in that field. A few months later, she became Mrs. Herbert Hoover.

39. Who were the first two presidents to win the Nobel Peace Prize?

A Rutherford B. Hayes and Benjamin Harrison

B Harry Truman and Lyndon Johnson

C Theodore Roosevelt and Woodrow Wilson

D John F. Kennedy and Barack Obama

Answer: C

Theodore Roosevelt won the Nobel Peace Prize in 1906 for having negotiated the peace treaty between Russia and Japan in 1905. Woodrow Wilson won in 1919 for his efforts in establishing the League of Nations after World War I.

40. What man who later became president was the first person to use a helicopter while campaigning for the U.S. Senate?

A Lyndon Johnson

B John F. Kennedy

C Richard Nixon

D George W. Bush

Answer:

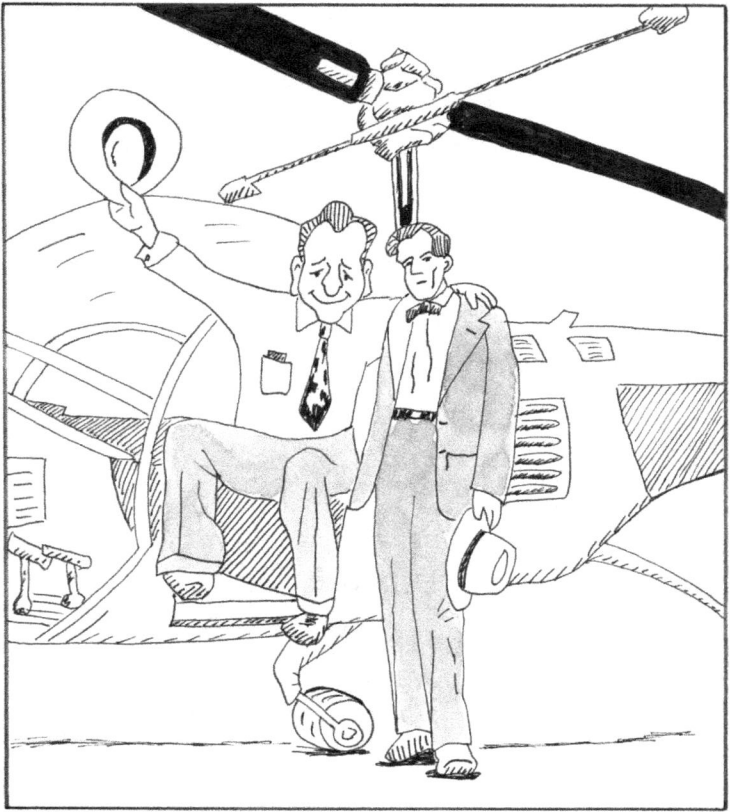

While running for a seat in the U.S. Senate in 1948, Lyndon Johnson became the first candidate for that position to use a helicopter to travel from one campaign event to another.

41. Who was the first president to address the nation in a live broadcast on coast-to-coast television?

A Franklin D. Roosevelt

B Dwight Eisenhower

C Harry Truman

D John F. Kennedy

Answer: C

On September 4, 1951, President Truman delivered a speech at the Japanese Peace Treaty Conference in San Francisco that was broadcast live across the nation. It was seen by thirty million people, the largest television audience ever at that time.

42. What president was such an avid golfer that he had a putting green installed on the White House grounds?

A Woodrow Wilson

B Dwight Eisenhower

C William Howard Taft

D Donald J. Trump

Answer:

President Eisenhower had the putting green installed on the White House lawn in 1954 with the help of the United States Golf Association. President Clinton had it moved to its current location.

43. **What president refused to accept an honorary degree from Oxford University?**

A Franklin D. Roosevelt

B Millard Fillmore

C Calvin Coolidge

D Gerald Ford

B

Answer:

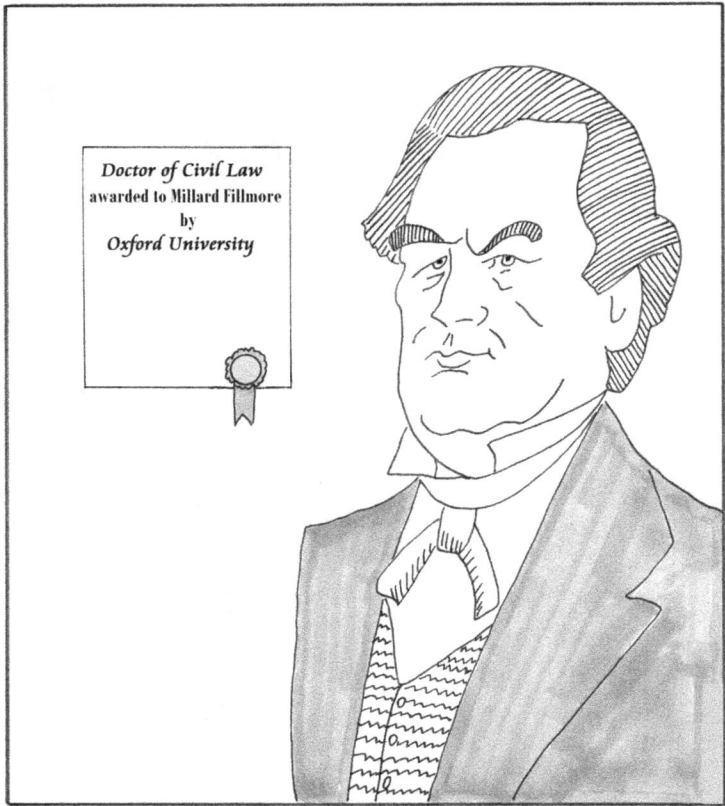

Doctor of Civil Law
awarded to Millard Fillmore
by
Oxford University

President Fillmore declined the offer of an honorary Doctor of Civil Law degree, saying "I had not the advantage of a classical education and no man should, in my judgment, accept a degree he cannot read."
(The degree was in Latin).

44. *Who was the only president who also served as Chief Justice?*

A William Howard Taft

B James Buchanan

C James A. Garfield

D John Quincy Adams

Answer:

Taft, who was president from
1909 to 1913, was appointed
Chief Justice in 1921 by President
Harding. He served until 1930.

45. What president holds the record for having the most children?

A James K. Polk

B William McKinley

C John Tyler

D Theodore Roosevelt

John Tyler had eight children with his first wife, Letitia Christian Tyler. After her death, he married Julia Gardiner, with whom he had seven more, for a total of fifteen.

46. What president once received a baby alligator as a gift and kept it for several months in the White House?

A John Quincy Adams

B Jimmy Carter

C Theodore Roosevelt

D Chester Alan Arthur

A

Answer:

Legend has it that John Quincy Adams received a baby alligator from the Marquis de Lafayette as a gift. He supposedly kept in for a few months in the bathtub in the East Room of the White House.

47. *What president was, in his younger days, a surveyor?*

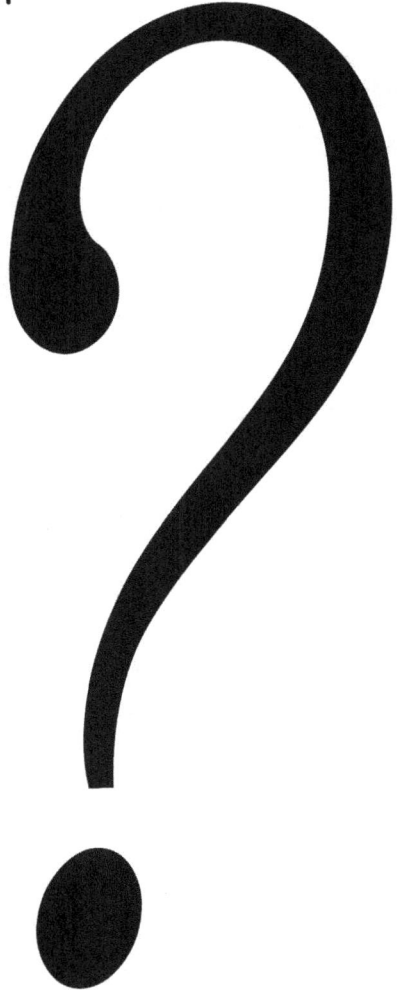

A Andrew Jackson

B George Washington

C James K. Polk

D John Adams

B Answer:

In 1749, at the age of seventeen, George Washington was appointed the county surveyor for Culpeper County, Virginia. In the three years he spent surveying, he completed 199 surveys of land on the western frontier of the American colonies.

48. During the 1960 presidential campaign, what did Jackie Kennedy do that no previous candidate's wife had ever done?

A Piloted an airplane

B Milked a cow in front of reporters

C Ran in the Boston Marathon

D Rode on a float in the Macy's Parade

Answer:

While her husband was campaigning in the Democratic primary in Wisconsin in 1960, Mrs. Kennedy posed for photographers while milking a cow.

Road to the White House

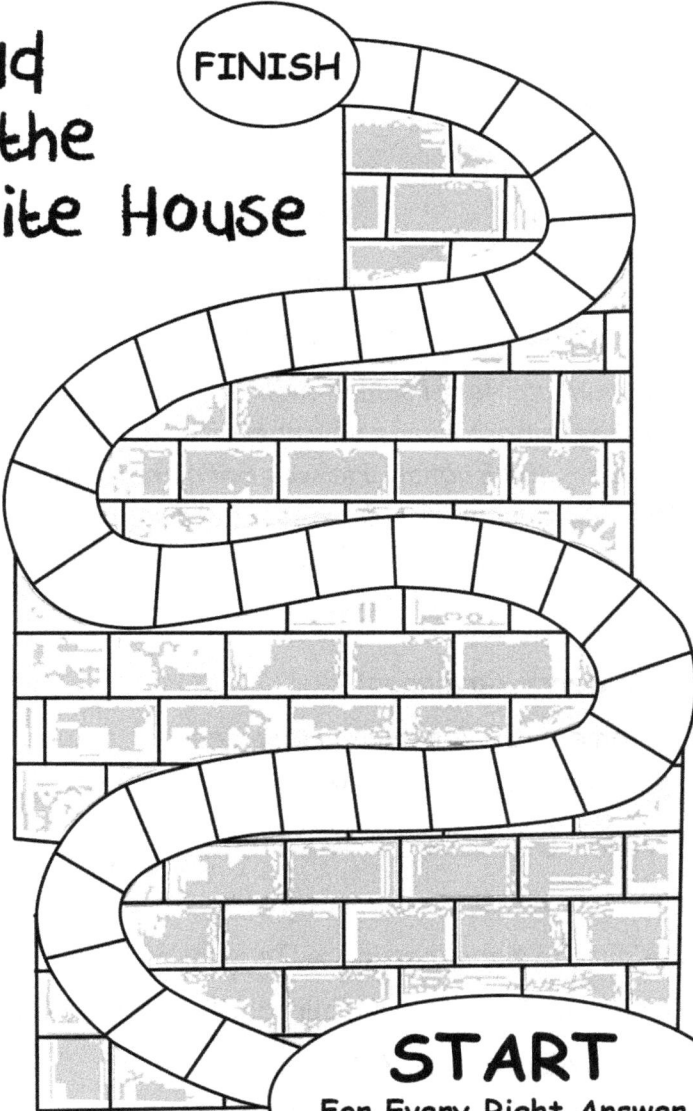

FINISH

START
For Every Right Answer
Check the Next Box

Jerry Cavanaugh

Jerry Cavanaugh is a former high school and middle school teacher, whose areas of expertise include history, psychology, and English. He was born and raised in Iowa, taught 35 years in the Davenport, Iowa, public schools, and now lives in Florida.

Also By Jerry Cavanaugh

Superwomen: 60 American Heroines

Presidential Tweets from Washington to Trump

Illustrivia: Illustrated Trivia Items (series of nine books)

Awesome to Absurd: Quotations to Guide Your Life...or Not

From Cairo to Kazakhstan: A Journal of Teaching Overseas

Two Years in Thailand: A Journal of Teaching Overseas

That's Why I'm Here: A Memoir

Caricatures by Cavanaugh: Senior Softball in the Villages

Inspiring the readers and writers of today and tomorrow!

Visit AimHiPress.com for more books and other products from AimHi Press
and the rest of the Newhouse Creative Group family!

Inspiring the readers and writers of today and tomorrow!

FREE Book for Subscribing to The NCG Narrative

Subscribe to our free newsletter, The NCG Narrative, to immediately receive a **FREE** eBook from Newhouse Creative Group.

Be the first to learn about NCG's newest releases, get behind the scenes of NCG, enter NCG Narrative exclusive contests and giveaways, and much more!

Subscribe today at NewhouseCreativeGroup.com

www.ingramcontent.com/pod-product-compliance
Lightning Source LLC
Chambersburg PA
CBHW060121050426
42448CB00010B/1981